CU00658442

NINE SERIES

Family Nam

Jenny Mitchell
Roy McFarlane
Zoë Brigley

Published by Nine Pens

2023

www.ninepens.co.uk

All rights reserved: no part of this book may be reproduced without the publisher's permission.

The rights of the authors Jenny Mitchell, Roy McFarlane and Zoë Brigley to be identified as the authors of this work has been asserted by them in accordance with the Copyright, Designs and Patents act 1988.

ISBN: 978-1-7391517-8-2

NS 008

Jenny Mitchell

Jenny Mitchell won the Gregory O'Donoghue Prize for a single poem, and the Poetry Book Awards for her second collection, *Map of a Plantation*, which is on the syllabus at Manchester Metropolitan University. The best-selling, prize-winning debut collection, *Her Lost Language*, is One of 44 Poetry Books for 2019 (Poetry Wales), and her latest collection, *Resurrection of a Black Man*, contains three prize-winning poems and is featured on the US podcast Poetry Unbound. She's won numerous competitions, is widely-published and recently performed at the Houses of Parliament.

For Black Women with Straightened Hair

I suffered, a hot comb searing scalp
like history or war to straighten out my kinks,
called *picky hair* – not fussy or meticulous.
Short and rough, a mess that's unacceptable,
according to the master's rules.

His mistress bids me brush her crackling mane,
one hundred strokes against black skin
until she's so relaxed, she can't undress herself.
I take the hooks from eyes, put moths inside her gown
to eat the crawling things that might destroy the cloth
at night.

She bids me kneel beside her bed to show a nappy crown.
Then bids again, says *Going, Going, Gone.*
I'll be worth more
if locks are straight. Good hair is close to white,
and needing that protection, I douse my head with lye,
raise welts, those self-inflicted brands. I suffered.

Black Hair

Entering the gallery, you'll see it in a case,
dark strands gathered close, size of a fist,
taken from a *Negroid head. Long-denigrated
in the West* a sign explains. *Known in the past
by several names – Bush, Wool, Nest.*

Nothing indicates why it was kept,
low temperature maintained, no air
beyond the seal, light so dim I must bend down
in order to look close. Did hair fall from a head
blighted by disease, gathered up like gold?

Was the owner male or female – afro worn as crown
or Black Power sign? Did a master pull it out,
punishment for burning crop? At night,
a woman screamed, scalp alarmed,
forced to make this sacrifice.

Is she screaming still, running through the woods,
bald patch covered up? Or standing firm
in jail, blood trickling down her face?
Does she demand her hair returned,
placed back on her head, a self-made wig?

People shuffle past the case to see
much grander sights – Turner's painting
of the *Zong*. Black hands raised above the foam.
Who cares to contemplate the hair
that could be mine – *Bush, Wool, Nest.*

lights in every window

grandfather drives her out that night. looms height & rum-inflated weight. walks grandmother. down the steps. of a two-room shack. both young. in what they'll call the golden times. her backwards. mouthing *no*. neighbours must not hear. *no* said again. it makes him raise his fist. block the light. except bright dots beneath her lids. she sprawls across the yard. he spits towards this woman. who will bear twelve children. four buried in the dirt. he slams the door. a lamp shakes dizzy in the window. he moves towards another drink. she crawls into their car. rust-filled. a missing wheel. insects nestle in the seats. crackle underfoot. windows glisten with the light. from a low half-moon. she sits proud. in the driver's seat. hands on the steering wheel. *go*. cracks an insect underneath her foot. *drive*. says the window pane. even if she could. this three-legged beast. would not go far. she sees bright lights ahead. leading to a house. she wants to call her own. with lights in every window. but it is a cat. lazing on the path. eyes light enough to lead this woman to another town. she hums. a steady engine sound. sings about the dawn. *i watch the sunlight shine through clouds*. her voice is soft and low. *i watch the sunset fade away*. the cat moves on. wide stretch beyond the path. grandmother huddles in the seat. grandfather opens up the door. calls her name. a light on in the neighbours' house. he calls again as if she is a dog. that must obey. go to this man. she hardly knows. as sun begins to rise.

Motherland

Morning breaks with her last breath, laid on a bed,
white as an unlined page, in contrast to her skin. Black
ink shows at the neck, more beneath the blouse –
strange tattooed self, whole body scarred till I look close.

There's all the world she's known – her lost Jamaican home,
lush land across wide shoulder blades. A stream flows
from her waist. Large breasts are hills. She climbs up
to the family crop. Her navel leads towards a road.

Bright lights along her gut, dim to an austere house.
She cleans for the white priest – *Master* to his flock.
He forces her to kneel, prayers not the ecstasy he seeks.
Her belly swells, the child born dead. She has to leave.

The image of a ship floats along one thigh. Waves crash
in cellulite on either hip beside White Cliffs of Dover.
A hotel near the Harrow Road displays this sign:
No blacks allowed. She has to clean ten rooms,

cannot board with the white maids. Hard to believe
religion is the first thing she seeks out. A Pentecostal church
where she meets Dad is etched across one shin,
his bold face on the next, beside a high rise flat.

Her nurse's uniform is traced along an inner thigh.
His goodbye note is stamped across both feet. She tiptoed
to old age, told me to bathe her when she died.
I didn't know she meant to wash her life away.

A Sudden Turn

The day before my mother dies
        lying on a sunken bed
                she wends a river through the room

                each word a steady flow
        whispered over rocks. Jagged shapes
lodged in her throat, prove obstacles. In time

a breeze helps rub them smooth, rushing
        to re-tell her life, battered on the shore
                forced along by currents

                she did not control. At night
                        her breath calm now, she takes
                                a sudden turn, aims towards
                the sun.

The Security Guard at Shopmore Says I Am a Thief

Grabs me from behind, rams against my back,
eyes brimming from his lids, saliva next to drool,
except I stop, throw down my bags, tell him to search.

He plunges elbows deep; nothing has been stolen.
Still, he shouts: *You're a thief. I saw you yesterday.*
My voice lies under his: *How dare you put your hands on me?*

He prowls to show his uniform has a cock inside.
There is rape, hard body says. *You're up against a wall.*
I tell him to move back. He bawls: *This woman is a thief.*

My voice is a loud hailer: *Liar. Don't tell lies.*
His voice is war: *Call the police. We'll have her sectioned.*
Did I forget to say I'm black, four times as likely to be held?

Women trapped at tills, sleepwalking down the aisles
look up to watch my madness led away in chains.
Defy or Die my motto, I stand firm, demanding an apology.

War looks down, offers me a cigarette – no word of a lie.
A pack of ten appears like a pipe of peace. He slurs, *Sorry if…*
I know it's time to leave, fake smile a medal on my face:

Sorry is surrender in abuse. I swagger even though it's false
to set off an alarm in war. He tries to show me rape again.
I dodge his growl, leave the battlefield. Cry on my way home.

One Bright Morning

It's happening today – a soon-to-be offender sneers,
points towards the only black boy in his class,
sends out a curse, aimed many times at the television
by his dad, flag held high when *One of them* appears,
sad-faced on a fragile boat, drifting out to sea.
Drown them all at birth, his father shouts.

Go back where you belong, his loyal son shouts
towards the new boy, fists about to strike, sneering
in the playground, urged on by his friends, a sea
of large white lads, most of whom nod off in class.
They feel such strength, puffed up, when it appears
to agitate the teachers, as if they are a gang on television.

The playground has become a scene on television,
where the new boy's chased, hunted down, shouting
out for help, arms raised, though not to fight – he appears
to drown. Cut to another scene – a coastguard sneers
when a boat tips in high waves, the loss of life classed
as a risk *These people* take by challenging the sea.

Back to the boy who's been engulfed, lost in a sea
of fists, feet aimed towards his head. On the television,
a gang might cheer to see the blood, but this rowdy class
of boys-turned-into-thugs steps back. One shouts,
Leave him alone – too late. The injured child sneers
with a rictus grin, hand salvaging his heart, so it appears.

No one breathes in the playground till they all appear –
teachers running for the young boy's life. A rushing sea
of them push back the gang, stare at the sneering
mask, a knife deep in the chest like on the television,
blade drowned up to the hilt. A teacher shouts,
Move back, herds the gang towards its class.

They cannot be contained as members of their class
call out, point towards one running boy. He appears
to be the owner of the knife. *No!* His father shouts
at the police. *It's not his fault. Blame the bloody sea
of refugees who swamp our land*. He is seen on television,
thrown into a van, as is his son, the same loyal sneer.

They're called a *Symbol of their class* with a sneer,
as if they shout the headlines, send out a constant sea
of blame till refugees appear as enemies on television.

Sister

after *Brother* by Dom Bury

He stands back – the coroner who has to examine
our big sister's body – open-mouthed to see
so many scars. Most of them are petrified.

Each one contains scrawled words, stamped hard.
One line is distinct – *I thought the best of men.*
A graze next to her mouth appears to have thin lips.

These words are etched along one side, *My first love
kissed then slapped.* Her left cheek's rosy
with a welt – *I begged him not to leave.*

The coroner takes steps, examines her right ear,
boxed deaf by a new man – *You're mine* pierced
on the lobe. Around her neck, a chain of words –

I'll never let you go. Eyes bulging now, the coroner
looks at her shoulder blades – *This bitch is a slag,*
scribbled underneath. *Don't forget you're mine.*

You deserve a slap. Let's give it one more try,
written on each breast. Close to the heart, cut deep,
the name of the last man who knocked her down –

a family kick-about. We tried to intervene. She cried,
Keep back, his foot aimed in the air. *It's all your fault*
met with its goal – three broken ribs. She laughed

too loud at some male neighbour's joke, agreed
it had been wrong, still lying on the ground.
That's how we found her, foetal in their home –

You've had your final chance carved down her spine.
Now we look on, arms useless at our sides. The coroner
bends to his task, records each word with care.

Delicately Wrought

This latest bruise is all my fault, skin delicate,
all shades of blood where he last gripped my arm,
pulled me from the door, tears shaken from my eyes.
It only really hurts to take a breath. A woman
with more stamina, more strength could stand
the pain when she is slammed against a wall.

It must be safe to press my back against the wall,
stand stiller than the wealth of roses delicately
wrought on paper so expensive I cannot stand
to see blood stains. It isn't a deep wound, my arm
cut by the door's sharp edge. A clumsy woman –
yes, he's right. I don't deserve the pity in his eyes.

Now he is walking up and down again, eyes
trained on the floor. If he comes close, the wall
must open up, miraculous, a door that's woman-
shaped. I'll escape the moment as it's delicate.
A breeze would help to sooth my face and arms.
Both are bruised – not badly – though I understand.

He didn't mean to grab so tight. If only I stood
still, had sense to know when he is on the edge, eyes
wild and strange as if I've never been held in his arms –
breath, once sweet, now sour on my face, a wall
made by his sweating bulk, not caring I am delicate,
manhandled like a piece of furniture, not a woman.

I wish he wouldn't say I am the type of woman
who must be kept inside the house. I couldn't stand
to lose my clothes. He picked up shoes so delicately,
said he'd clean them all. It was odd but his eyes
glared so I dare not argue, pressed against the wall
until he left the house, shoes bundled in his arms.

He set a fire on the lawn, stood close as both arms
hurled the shoes, a high-pitched laugh like a man
who's lost his grip. Now he's coming close, a wall
that wants to knock me down. I pretend to understand
why money has to be transferred to him. His eyes
look kind but even more surprising, his touch is delicate.

Then he slaps my arm, leads me to the desk. I delicately
lift the pen, edge back against the wall as he stands
close. *Woman, sign at once.* A quick punch to the eye.

Roy McFarlane

Roy McFarlane is a Poet, Playwright and former Youth & Community Worker born in Birmingham of Jamaican parentage, living in Brighton. He's the National Canal Laureate, a former Birmingham Poet Laureate and one of the Bards of Brum performing in the Opening Ceremony for Birmingham Commonwealth Games 2022.

His debut collection, *Beginning With Your Last Breath,* was followed by *The Healing Next Time,* shortlisted for the Ted Hughes award and longlisted for the Jhalak Prize. His third collection *Living by Troubled Waters* (Nine Arches Press 2022) is out now.

Past Midnight

It's past midnight as I lay my head on my pillow.
I hear a sound, a familiar melody to my jazz ears, Chet Baker.
And usually when I lean on the door of sleep, I'll fall right in –
late night revellers, seagulls squawking and the rumblings of thunder
barely move me but tonight I'm pulled and lulled, and find
I'm at the edge of my windowsill, curtains eased open
I press my head against the window pane, to know this sound.

Below, one floor adjacent to me, an apartment is lit up like a stage
in the darkness, someone, a woman is in a dreamy state, holding
her body in a sweet embrace. Window wide open, she spins
and sings, wearing barely anything and a smile, as if nothing matters,
right here, right now. And I remember Chet Baker in an interview,
rasping, rugged voice, *I don't think life is really worth all the pain*
and effort and struggling, if you don't have someone that you love very much.

And perhaps in Amsterdam Chet Baker *fell in love too terribly hard*
for love to ever last, where he died and sirens; heroin and cocaine sung
their unearthly song. Myths declare "sirens are ones who bind or entangle
through magic song." And she sees me, continues her dance, an apparition
before my eyes. And believe me, I desire to open this window, step across
the void. But tethered by prudency and warning cries of seagulls,
I return to my pillow and fall deep into an ocean of sleep.

Call me by my name

1.

Hurricanes have always followed our family from the day we arrived – enslaved, our true names taken away from us – on these islands in the Caribbean Sea.

2.

Anything characterised by a turmoil or force, suggestive of a hurricane.
These are the islands that adopted us. Uprooted from another land, we were planted in hostility; lands we weren't given, but bloody in fruits, baptised in seasons of hurricanes.

3.

Taino (the original people of the land) lived in *yucayequues*, led by *Cacike*. Hear their tongue, their lyrics in *barbeque, canoe, cassava, guava, manatee,* people of *Xaymacca* the land of wood and water, they knew how to name their gods, a child so mischievous its strength tore islands apart…
Huracan, Huracan, Huracan.

4.

The British anglicized the name of *Huracan* every time he returned, reborn, renamed; Charlie, Gilbert, Ivan, Dean and many more.

5.

Our first known meeting with *Huracan* – the one they called
Hurricane Charlie – my mother remembers of how the sky
was blue before it turned celestial red, of how people moved
to a bigger house for safety, of how they prayed, of how they
woke to see banana and orange trees laying prostrate to an
island god who had passed over the land, of how rivers
swelled, of how people lamented and breadfruit roasting
incensed the air.

6.

Always be kind to your Zemis (gods of both sexes) serve them
casava bread and they'll protect you from hurricanes
according to Taino legend. Over 4000 miles away from
Hurricane Dean, my children in the eye of a divorce are
holidaying with their mother in Jamaica in an oncoming
storm and I back in England watching CNN and making fried
dumplings with ackee and saltfish praying the Holy Ghost
(god of both sexes) will look after them.

7.

Grace Nicholls talked of a hurricane
that came visiting a British Isle,
came looking for her Windrush Children.
Talk to me Hurucan
Talk to me Oya
Talk to me Shango

Haibun for *The Fields*

for Ismael Zechariah McFarlane (my life father)

My wonderland, my place of adventures, green domain
hidden behind terraced houses on one side and the local
factory on the other side, steel stockholders warning us not to
enter with steel meshed fencing, barbed wire and the sound
of unearthly machines carrying heavy loads. There in that
space, a land would magic into existence in the evening,
weekends and summer holidays. Teenagers seeped in from
alleys, broken fences, back gardens and side roads. A space
where all people of colour came to play, boys in the centre
and girls at the edge of our desires. There we bruised, tussled,
kicked the ball, knocked the ball in the height of summer – tall
trees at the edge would rustle in the lightest of breeze – only
to be interrupted by *catch it* followed by a chorus, *he dropped
it!* There the smell of corned beef and fried dumpling from
home enticed you but you hold on to the evening wrestling
the dusk on the border. Young girls would join in, holding
you just a little while longer, the shared lick of an ice cream,
chocolate flakes dipped in vanilla white. Mother's calling you
from the backyard with dusk still held at arm's length you'd
risk that last taste, the forbidden bite before your father's
voice boomed like steel rods dropping on concrete floor,
causing the domain to disappear, folding before your very
eyes; legs running, running…

*We longed for the dirt
our friend; the soil our comfort,
we the children of The Fields.*

Isle of Skye

for Cee

We visited the small bay with a beach
you'd miss in a blink of an eye, if flying by.
We watched a ferry inject life,
feeding and taking from the winged Isles.

Artiste abode, cafes and shanty shacks,
white dreadlocked hippies pointed
to hidden lairs and trails whilst high
on the sweet scent that filled the air.

We looked as far as the eye could see
where blue waters and cerulean skies
held hands somewhere over the horizon
and behind us the hills kissed the heavens.

We should never have left the Isle
of oystercatchers on coral beeches,
water playground of seals and sea eagles
for in the blink of a lifetime, I lost it all
                    when we left the Isle of Skye.

The Valley of the Rising Sun

A thing of beauty is a joy forever

Endymion – John Keats

Two years to make and a hundred souls
built Galton Valley, where water divides
a summit and flows under bridge
of iron, casting a shadow of beauty
under Helios' watchful eye, a joy forever to be seen.

These wonders outlive us; a bridge that frames the sky,
a canopy over this Eden where wild berries tempt you,
foxglove in purple soothe you and sunflowers
at the water's edge look lovingly at Helios
riding his chariot across the skies.

A bee blind drunk with summer nectar
legless buzzing on a bricked towpath.
And young men *nos* on balloons filled
with laughing gas, giddy and dizzy
and you pray they make it through the solstice
without turning into sunflowers along the way.

**nos: Nitrous Oxide slows down your brain and your body's response,
and the effects of the drug varies depending on how much has been inhaled.*

Lords of the Earth

Poseidon, god of water; his name means "husband of the earth" or "lord of the earth."

- Britanica.com

for Roger and The Men of Ellesmere Yard

These men who know waters
when embankments disappear
where water doesn't stand still
they manage and manipulate
                the flow of water.

These "lords of the earth"
will walk across lands
to cut and remove fallen trees
or carry sheep across water.

Usher the dead from boats gone adrift
guide the parasuicide tied to aqueducts.
These lords know the danger of water
have been pulled under and crushed
                by heavy water.

Remember; water is never level,
know your highs and lows,
feed the canals, feed the reservoir
and when storms come let water through.

These "husbands of the earth,"
emergency responders
and controllers of waters

will hold bridges up
and if need be, pull them down.

And people will sleep safely on water
and know the nudge of quiet streams.

The House that Lilith Made: Sliding Doors

Wildcats shall meet with hyenas, goat-demons shall call to each other; there too Lilith shall repose, and find a place to rest.

Isaiah 34:14 NRSV

> The door slides open –
> an aroma so light
> suffuses my senses,
> a burgundy sweetness.

Doors are never closed but they may slide silently
for moments of healing because god can be found
in the still small voice of a woman crying.
Here, walls are soft soaking up the tears of yesterday.

In the inner courtyard there are no ceilings,
women will stretch and not be disfigured
by their own excellence and existence
women will not stoop or bend, dusting debris

of men's insecurities off their shoulders.
Women will reach their tired limbs to the sky,
glove their hands in silk clouds and reach beyond,
plucking stars from the velvet womb of the universe.

> Women run from room
> to room, laughing, heads
> flung back. The music
> in the walls responds to touch.

The House that Lilith Made: The Garden

In the house that Lilith made, there'll be dancing
some having danced on the bones of men,
heel in eye sockets, jaw bones becoming maracas
whilst cavorting in a whirlwind of red dust
and in the settling of the storm, women will rise,
wrap themselves in robes of their own making and rise.

> I am a sojourner amongst
> these women of all shades
> from magnolia to blackberry,
> carrying their size and shapes
> without burden of gaze.

...bleeding will be found in the gardens, the beginning
and ending, where lakes will draw women across time.

In the gardens of Lilith there will be babies,
because babies know the scent of unwantedness.

Babies who were born in misfortune, incubated
in the beating and bruising of suffering mothers.

Under the light of the moon, they will crawl
and play with wildcats, laughing with hyenas.

After hearing of Plath likening despair to an owl sitting
on her chest, I find you in Fuseli's *The Nightmare*

for my birth father with no name

The woman in deep sleep.
Almost hovering above her head
body stretched, draped, arched,
a creature sits on her abdomen
abdodere, the place of hiding.

This is where I find you, hiding deep
talons clenching a constricting heart
my heart desires to know you, daddy.

Are you the sire that haunts me?
Dark and headless in the background
the young man inside cries to know you, daddy.

Are you the despair, the fire and the fury?
A volcano that erupts without notice,
the anger that boils within to know you, daddy

don't you realise you're supposed to be
my legacy, my jazz funk, my spirituals,
my way into my history, my testimony,
my beginning and my ending,
the weight to know you, daddy.

Zoë Brigley

Zoë Brigley is editor of *Poetry Wales*, a poetry editor for Seren Books, and she lectures in the English department at the Ohio State University. She has three poetry collections, all of which were PBS Recommendations, most recently *Hand & Skull* (Bloodaxe, 2019). Her recent poetry chapbooks include *Aubade After A French Movie* (Broken Sleep, 2020) and *Into Eros* (Verve 2021). She was editor of *100 Poems to Save the Earth* (Seren 2021; edited with Kristian Evans). She published a collection of nonfiction essays *Notes from a Swing State* (Parthian 2019) and a collaborative nonfiction pamphlet with Kristian Evans, *Otherworlds* (Broken Sleep, 2021). She is winner of an Eric Gregory Award for the best British poets under 30 and was listed for the Dylan Thomas Prize for the best international writers under 40.

Wollstonecraft

a hyena in petticoats
                —Horace Walpole describes Mary Wollstonecraft

A family name from the Saxons, *wulfstan,* or
wolf stone, set unusually with *craft* referring
(for West Saxons) not to a skill but physical
strength and might, *the power of the wolf stone,*
a name that may derive from the Vikings.
This name redolent of *wylfenne geðohtas,* wolfish
thoughts feminine in nature; of *waelwulfas,* wolves
that slaughter in battle; of the devil himself
who wears a wolf's head, or the wolf who lay
in grandmother's bed; of King Hywel Da whose
price for a wolf was eight pence, and who paid
Saxon tributes in wolf-skins. What can a she-wolf
do but survive? No matter the names that seek
to make animal and woman less than human.

The Men of the Family Wollstonecraft

She comes from a long line of men named
Edward Wollstonecraft. The eldest Edward
is her grandfather: master weaver and later
landlord of Spitalfields. The next Edward is
her father, another weaver who longed to be
a gentleman farmer, prone to drunken rages,
profligate, quick to hit his wife and dogs,
subject to his daughter's contempt, always
"a good hater". And her eldest brother,
Edward or Ned, light of her father's eye:
he will despise his sister's notoriety so much,
he'll emigrate to Australia, granted 10,000
acres on the Shoalhaven River, on land
still inhabited by the Jerrinja people.

Original Stories from Real Life*

Consider: The treatment of animals. The bee.
The lark's nest. The difference between them
and man. Brutality punished. A man confined
in the Bastille. Lying. Truth. Small duties.
A tulip. The rose. A summer evening's
amusement. A family of haymakers. A storm.
Fear of death. A cottage. A shipwrecked sailor
and a dog named Pompey. Inconvenience.
Indulgence. The danger of delay. A mansion
in ruins. The village schoolmistress. Servants.
Dignity. Trifling omissions and undermined
affection. Character. Benefits of bodily pain.
Employment. Idleness. The cultivation of fancy.
Happiness. Resignation. Moonlight. Prayer.

---

* A found poem from the chapter summaries of Mary Wollstonecraft's
*Original Stories from Real Life with Conversations Calculated to Regulate the
Affections and Form the Mind to Truth and Goodness,* written for young girls,
first published 1788.

Feminism is For Everybody

—bell hooks

I.*

If the story sounds melodramatic, that's because
it is – as Godwin tells it. So close to Christmas,
the miracle of wood bears her creaking across
the swallowing waves, but the English captain
refuses the spent French sailors, their ship
foundering, seamen crushed by hunger.
What did she say to persuade? Did she call
on God? Or charity? On compassion? Or
the brute authority of other men at home,
the threat of being *called to severe account*.
Not just the rights of women but the rights
of men, the rights of the human. *She had*
the satisfaction to reflect, that these men
in question owed their lives to her interposition.

---

* *20th December 1785: Mary embarks on the journey home by ship from*
Portugal to England.

II.

After *Mary: A Fiction* (1787)

She learns so much, but still there are
things beyond her understanding. In *Mary,*
she writes, *I will work, do anything rather*
than be a slave, but she does not know
what that means. When she compares
a white woman trapped by marriage
to African slaves, she is imagining
the life of a black woman as very
like her own, the differences flattened
by the lack in what she does not know:
bladed monotony, a horror of whiteness,
the empty ledger of a white man's eyes.
Ten years earlier, Phyllis Wheatley wrote:
Let virtue reign and then accord our prayers.

Letter to Gilbert Imlay[*]

my love do – not shut your – heart be my – best
support feel as – affectionate as – I do when
you read these – letters I am – afraid I vex – you
my whole – happiness depends on – you I play
and laugh with – the little – girl pressing her
to my – bosom she looked – so like you but
your real face – not your commercial one – if
our affection is – mutual act – accordingly dear
Imlay – how you love – to fly – dropping down
in a new – world cold and strange – and how
am – I to stifle – my resentment at fresh – proofs
of your – indifference my friend – my dear friend
examine yourself I – want not vulgar – comfort
I want your – heart that gone there is – nothing more

---

[*] Found poem from Mary Wollstonecraft's letters (December 1793-November 1795), some unanswered, to the father of her daughter and common law husband, Gilbert Imlay. They would never be lovers again.

The Last Word to Gilbert Imlay

*I am weary of travelling – yet seem to have no home – no resting place to
look to. – I am strangely cast off. – How often, passing through the rocks, I
have thought, 'But for this child, I would …. never open my eyes again!'*
—Letter from Mary Wollstonecraft to Gilbert
Imlay, September 6, 1795

No passion but coolly reasonable: the rationale
of a human who seeks to leap from a burning
building. First survived: laudanum's queasy fall
into nothingness. Now, by drowning. No need
for an audience. She has rowed from Battersea
to Putney Bridge, stood in the rain and waited,
daring the dark river: not death by flame but
by the sharp slap of cold water, but she under-
estimates the pain of gulping down the Thames
instead of air, and how the body betrays her
by fighting to stay alive, her dress sunk to
an anchor. She is slipping and yet… and yet…
Alive and awake in her convalescent bed,
Now I am to you a person dead, she says.

We Did Not Marry
-William Godwin*

And when she first calls on him, it's April
in Somerstown, and the leaves, blooms,
buds shiver on the trees. To her, he is
morning and the dream and the waking.
And by August, when they cannot stop
wanting one another, he is an apple held
in her palm, its sweet, cool weight. How
he won't let anyone box her. He does not
stand to be cultivated. He is a mountain
in sleep, his closed fist against his cheek.
What is he – lover, collaborator, equal –
but everything she asked for and more?
He is the morning and the dream: he is
the wakening. He is an apple in her hand.

---

* William Godwin and Mary Wollstonecraft began an intense affair in 1796,
deciding at least at first not to marry, the admission of which was scandalous
when Godwin wrote his late wife's biography.

At Newington Green Unitarian

It is certain that no animal brings forth its young with as much difficulty,
pain, and danger as a woman.
            —Letter from Joseph Clark to Richard Price, June 9th 1785

She won't recall the itch of lace at her collar, how
her behind ached on the hard pew, only Price
speaking: this is happiness, such beginnings, his
attention to her, a man thin and modest, rider
of a half-blind horse, dressed in black, in sympathy
with birds and women. In his defence, she'll write:
The world is not yet civilized enough. From Price,
she learns that liberty is deciding for oneself.
As yet unlived: the limits of women's freedom,
when her doctor misses the placenta curdling
the womb – it will kill her before she can know
her newborn. So much for self-determination.
Still, the arched windows are full of light as
Price says: *You cannot hold the world in darkness.*

Acknowledgments:

Jenny Mitchell

These poems have previously been published by, or in association with, Nine Pens, perhappened, Secret Chords – Best of the Folklore Prize, Bedford Poetry Competition 2021 Anthology, SMEOP – Urban issue, A Question of Identity – Arts Richmond Poetry Prize, the Ironbridge Prize, the Ware Prize, the Binstead Prize.

Roy McFarlane

Haibun for *The Fields,* First published in Setumag as part of their British Working-Class Poets series, USA www.setumag.com: Call me by my name, *Across Borders, an anthology of new poetry from the commonwealth,* Verve Poetry Press, 2022: The Valley of the Rising Sun, written as part of the Equinox series during my tenure as National Canal Laureate: Lords of the Earth, commissioned poem for the men of Ellesmere Yard, the oldest working boatyard in England during my tenure as National Canal Laureate: The House that Lilith Made, a previous, longer, version won second place in the Poetry Wales Competition 2020 selected by Pascale Petit: After hearing of Plath likening despair to an owl sitting on her chest, I find you in Fuseli's The Nightmare, Ed Sarah Corbett & Ian Humphreys, *After Sylvia: Poems And Essays In Celebration Of Sylvia Plath,* Nine Arches Press, 2022

Zoë Brigley

These poems are indebted to the scholarly and biographical works on Mary Wollstonecraft by Lyndall Gordon, Pamela Clemit, Gary Kelly, Claudia L. Johnson, Chris Jones, Moira Ferguson, Janet M. Todd and Gina Luria Walker, as well as William Godwin's account of his wife's life. An early version of 'At Newington Green Unitarian' was published in *Free Verse: Poems for Richard Price,* ed. Damian Walford Davies and Kevin Mills (Seren, 2023).

Milton Keynes UK
Ingram Content Group UK Ltd.
UKHW012157031123
431852UK00004B/299